# Kids'

## magnetic poetry®

## Book and Creativity Kit

by

## Dave Kapell
## & Sally Steenland

Workman Publishing
New York

We gratefully acknowledge contributors to this book for permission
to print their poems. Every effort has been made to contact contributors. If any required credits have been omitted, it is completely
unintentional, and we will gladly correct any omissions in reprints.

Library of Congress Cataloging-in-Publication Data
Kapell, Dave. The kids' magnetic poetry book and creativity kit / by
Dave Kapell & Sally Steenland.
p. cm.
Summary: This activity-filled kit explains the concepts of rhythm and
rhyme, figures of speech, alliteration, and onomatopoeia, and how they
are used to create poetry.
ISBN 0-7611-1357-6
1. Poetry—Authorship—Juvenile literature. 2. Children's poetry,
American. [1. Poetry—Authorship. 2. American poetry.] I. Steenland,
Sally. II. Title.
PN1059.A9K37 1998   808.1—dc21   98-26128 CIP AC

Workman books are available at special discounts when purchased
in bulk for premiums and sales promotions as well as for fund-raising
or educational use. Special editions can also be created to specification.
For details, contact the Special Sales Director at the address below.

Workman Publishing Company, Inc.
708 Broadway
New York, NY  10003-9555
http://www.workmanweb.com

Printed in China
First printing September 1998
10 9 8 7 6 5 4 3 2 1

for | my | mom | my |
dad | d | y |
& | sister |
D | K |


for | Miya | & | Noah |
Maggie | & | Will |
S | S |

## thanks  !

Many books were invaluable sources as we developed the writing exercises. *Wishes, Lies, and Dreams* by Kenneth Koch was filled with great ideas, as were many, many books from The Teachers & Writers Collaborative—too many to list here! Also helpful was *The Practice of Poetry,* edited by Robin Behn and Chase Twichell, and *In the Palm of Your Hand,* by Steve Kowit.

Thanks to all the teachers and students who shared with us their ideas and poems.

"Life Doesn't Frighten Me" from *And Still I Rise* by Maya Angelou. Copyright © 1978 by Maya Angelou. Reprinted by permission of Random House, Inc. "We Real Cool," by Gwendolyn Brooks © 1991 in the book *Blacks,* published by Third World Press, 1991. "City" by Langston Hughes, from *Golden Slippers: An Anthology of Negro Poetry,* by Arna Bontemps, ed. Copyright © 1944 by Knopf. Reprinted by permission of Knopf. "Now listen, you watermelons" is reprinted from *Ten Poems by Issa,* English versions by Robert Bly, Floating Island Press, Pt. Reyes, California, 1992. Copyright 1992 by Robert Bly. Reprinted with his permission. "The Garden Hose" by Beatrice Janosco. Copyright © 1966 by Beatrice Janosco. "Thistles" by Karla Kuskin. Copyright © 1964, renewed 1992 by Karla Kuskin. Reprinted by permission of S©ott Treimel New York. "Halfway Down" by A. A. Milne, from *When We Were Very Young* by A. A. Milne. Illustrations by E. H. Shepard. Copyright © 1924 by E. P. Dutton, renewed 1952 by A. A. Milne. Used by permission of Dutton Children's Books, a division of Penguin Putnam Inc. "Night Creature" from *Little Raccoon and Poems From the Woods* in *Something New Begins* by Lilian Moore. Copyright © 1967, 1969, 1972, 1975, 1980, 1982 by Lilian Moore. Reprinted by permission of Marian Reiner for the author. "Permit Me to Warn You" by Charles Reznikoff, from *By the Waters of Manhattan.* Copyright © 1959 by Charles Reznikoff. Reprinted by permission of New Directions Publishing Corp. "Buffalo Dusk" from *Smoke and Steel* by Carl Sandburg. Copyright © 1920 by Harcourt Brace and Company and renewed 1948 by Carl Sandburg, reprinted by permission of the publisher. "Our Mom's a Real Nice Mom But She Can't Cook" is reprinted with the permission of Atheneum Books for Young Readers, an imprint of Simon and Schuster Children's Publishing Division from *Sad Underwear and Other Complications* by Judith Viorst. Text copyright © 1995 Judith Viorst.

# contents

# Twinkling Toenails

A Foreword by Judith Viorst

What are we to do with all of these thoughts that buzz in our brains, and with all of these feelings stirring our hearts? One good thing to do with them is make poems. We can take the stuff inside us—the nice and not nice, the worried and joyful, the loving and the lonely and the lost—and find the words to talk about them, words that tell exactly what we mean. I like what a poet named Samuel Taylor Coleridge once said was the difference between prose and poetry. He didn't say that prose doesn't rhyme and poetry has to rhyme. (No it doesn't.) He didn't say that prose could be plain but that poetry has to be beautiful. (No it doesn't.) He didn't say that prose could be funny and that poetry has to be serious. (No it doesn't.) He said instead that while prose is "words in their best order," poetry is "the best words in their best order."

So here you are, with your feelings and thoughts—and a batch of fine words to put in their best order. Are you experiencing a magnetic attraction? Maybe it's time for you to make a poem.

But wait. Hold on. Have you read any poetry lately? Reading poetry helps us to make poems. It reminds us of the different shapes and sounds a poem can have.

It reminds us that poems can be doors to places we've never been before or mirrors of what we already are and know. It reminds us that poems can be frisky and free or, like a puzzle or game, bound by rules that challenge rather than choke us. It reminds us, too, that a poem can be about anything—yes, anything—and that there's nothing too weird or too ordinary, too terrible or too silly, to put in a poem.

Reading poems reminds us that sometimes the most surprising words can be "the best words," that the most amazing orders can be "their best order." And it also reminds us that, as a poet named Dylan Thomas once said, poetry "makes you laugh, cry, prickle, be silent, makes your toenails twinkle."

What kind of poetry makes *your* toenails twinkle?

Maybe you think that there isn't a poem in the world that could possibly make your toenails twinkle. I find it hard to believe that this is true. Not every poem is for everyone, but somewhere on this planet (perhaps in this book) is a poem (perhaps a whole lot of poems) just for you. And when you discover a poem that seems to be written just for you it's because the writer of that poem has crossed the space that separates the two of you and—gasp! giggle! weep! sigh! twinkle!—has made a connection.

But it doesn't have to be a direct connection.

Instead, we can feel exactly what a poem intends us to feel without being tapped on the shoulder and *told* to feel it. A poem often says what it means in roundabout ways.

"We are alone and small, and heaven is high; / Quintillion worlds have burst and left no trace" is how poet Peter Viereck says, "It's scary out here." "We cannot cage the minute/Within its nets of gold" is how poet Louis MacNeice says, "We cannot stop time." As Lewis Carroll, the man who wrote *Alice's Adventures in Wonderland,* once advised:

> *When you are describing*
> *A shape, or sound, or tint;*
> *Don't state the matter plainly,*
> *But put it in a hint;*
> *And learn to look at all things*
> *With a sort of mental squint.*

I think that most poets, when trying to put the best words in their best order, are doing so with a sort of mental squint.

And so, when you're ready to go make a poem, you may want to do some squinting. You probably ought to do some listening, too, hearing how the sound of a word can count just as much as its meaning, hearing how its rhythm and music are part of the deepest meaning of a poem. In the special language of poetry the way words sound to the ear can make the heartaches more achy, the shivers more shivery, the jubilation more jubilant, can help us—as poet Robert Herrick does—to actually *hear* Julia's voice, "So smooth, so sweet, so silv'ry . . . /Melting melodious words"; and can play the jazzy syncopated beat of poet Gwendolyn Brooks's "We real cool. We/Left school. We . . ."

Do you know that you can play music by putting the best
words in their best order?

And do you also know how completely delicious it can be
to make a poem?

Now it's true that poets will talk about the blood and
sweat and tears of poetry writing. But that isn't the only
way poets write poems. A poet named Kenneth Koch
once said—and I certainly agree—that it's "such a pleasure to say things, and such a special kind of pleasure to
say them as poetry."

Writing a poem can make you feel as if a cork has been
pulled from the top of your head.

It can make you feel that you've found a home for your
heart.

It can make you feel you've discovered a secret self that
lives inside you.

It can sometimes even make your toenails twinkle.

# Welcome to Words

A poem needs words like you need air—to live. But not just any words. Poems need the best words you can think of—scary, funny, angry, silly, lonely, hopeful words.

How can you find words like that?

Listen to all the sounds surrounding you. Pay attention to what's inside your head. Look around at the outside world and you'll find the words you need.

Don't give up if your poem doesn't sound quite right the first time.

Think of a basketball player shooting hoops. One ball clangs off the rim, while another bounces off the backboard. But after lots of practice, the ball soars through the air and *swissshhhh!* It goes right in. And everyone who's watching says, *"yesss!"*

When you find the best words for your poem, it'll feel like magic. The words will do whatever you want them to do. They'll dunk, float, slip, and fly into poems so surprising and bright that everyone who reads them will say, *"yesss!"*

1

# The One-Two-Three of Words

First things first: Words are made up of sounds. And poems are made up of words. The sound of a word matters a lot when you're writing a poem. For instance, the words **rock** and **stone** mean the same thing. So do **small** and **little**. But even though their meanings are identical, their sounds are different.

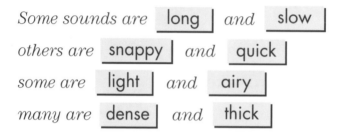

*Some sounds are* long *and* slow
*others are* snappy *and* quick
*some are* light *and* airy
*many are* dense *and* thick

Great sound effects—that's what you're after in your poems. And you can get them by picking words not only for their meaning but also for their sound.

Check the Toolbox (on page 6) to find the names for some of these sound effects. But you don't need to know the names to write poetry.

**1.** A word's **sound** will often give you a clue to its meaning. Take the word **buzz** and say it out loud. Stretch out the ending, and you've got a cruising bumblebee. Or say the word **sigh**. Say it soft and low, and you've just done it (sighed, that is).

ACTIVITY | **sound-fx**

Grunt, howl, yell, screech, roar, sneer, cry, giggle. Make any sound—it doesn't matter what.

Now, take your sound and turn it into a word. For example, "grrr" can become "growl." "Waaa" can turn into "wail." Here are some more examples:

"rrrff" (like a dog barking) turns into "rough."

"mmowww" (like you've got a stomach-ache) turns into "moan."

"brrr" (like you're shivering) turns into "breeze."

See how noises can shift into words? And see how their sound is a clue to their meaning?

Think up other words that sound like what they mean. Here's a start:

tickle | groan | creak | gargle | moo | chirp | quack

Try writing a poem using some of the words you've just thought up.

# 2.

Sometimes poems contain words that **start** with the same letter. Here's one using only words that start with **b**.

because | bad | boy | s | bite | book | s |

big | bubble | breakfast | s |

bounce | back |

---

**ACTIVITY** | **letter lineup**

Choose a group of word tiles that start with the same letter. You can pick any letter you like—A or T or S, for instance— just make sure you get enough words to play with. See if you can write a poem using only those words. Don't worry about making sense or sounding silly; put the words together any way you like.

Change your poem by adding words that start with different letters. You can move the b words around, add some, or drop some.

why | are | boy | s | big | ? |
because |

the | bubble | s | they | bite |

for | breakfast | blow |

up | inside |

Another thing about sound: Just because words begin with the same sound doesn't mean they begin with the same letter. Think about these:

sink and city , cat and kind , know and nasty

**3.** And not just beginning sounds: The **middle** of words can sound the same, too. Listen to these pairs of words: **light** and **time**, **monkey** and **bug**, **whisper** and **little.** See how they sound the same in the middle? Pick out some word tiles whose middle sounds are similar. What kind of feeling do the sounds suggest? Tired? Hurried? Sad? Are they fast or slow?

ACTIVITY **middle match**

Try writing a poem in which the middle sounds of the words are similar. See if you can match the mood of the poem with the sounds. What kind of feeling have you created?

## THISTLES

*Thirty thirsty thistles*
*Thicketed and green*
*Growing in a grassy swamp*
*Purple-topped and lean*
*Prickly and thistly*
*Topped by tufts of thorns*
*Green mean little leaves on them*
*And tiny purple horns*
*Briary and brambly*
*A spiky, spiney bunch of them.*
*A troop of bright-red birds came by*
*And had a lovely lunch of them.*

This poem by KARLA KUSKIN has all kinds of sound effects in it.

### sound effects

**1.** Onomatopoeia (On-oh-mah-tuh-PEE-ah)
**2.** Alliteration (Ah-lit-er-AY-shun)
**3.** Assonance (AS-sun-nence)
**4.** Homonyms (HOM-uh-nims)

## Sense and Nonsense

**4.** Okay, so each word has a particular sound. But it's got **meaning**, too. Probably more than one. Even simple words like **can** or **lap** or **spring** mean more than one thing.

ACTIVITY | **tricky bits**

Look up the word run in the dictionary. How many meanings are there? See how many words you can think of that mean more than one thing. Here's a start:

club | back | fresh | hard | bug | mean

Write a poem using some of these "tricky" words. Here's an example:

I | mean

that | bug | was | mean

so | I | whack | ed

its | back | with | a | club

it | whack | ed | me | back

I | said | you're | fresh

and | ate | it

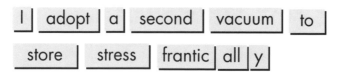

I | adopt | a | second | vacuum | to | store | stress | frantic | all | y

NATHAN KIRCHHOFFER (age 10)

But there's no rule saying every word has to mean something. Some words are nonsense. You can make up a nonsense word by squishing different sounds together—a little bit of this and that—and liking what comes out. Nonsense words often show up in poems.

**JABBERWOCKY**

*'Twas brillig, and the slithy toves*
*Did gyre and gimble in the wabe:*
*All mimsy were the borogoves,*
*And the mome raths outgrabe.*

LEWIS CARROLL, who wrote
*Alice's Adventures in
Wonderland,* also wrote
this nonsense poem.

ACTIVITY | **s e n s e   o r   n o n ?**

Make up **a word and put it into a poem. Come up with a meaning for your word, but before you tell, ask your friends to guess what they think the word means. Here are some possibilities:**

groot | torlet | snoat | yaner

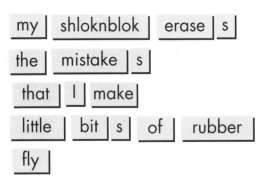

my | shloknblok | erase | s
the | mistake | s
that | I | make
little | bit | s | of | rubber
fly

L. J. KOSTICK (age 10)

## MagPo's Way with Words

Words have roots, just like plants. They also have branches—letters you can attach to the root that make the word grow. For instance, if you take the root **sweat** and add **er**, you get **sweater**. Stick another **er** onto **crack** and you get **cracker**. Put one more **er** onto **flow** and you've got **flower**. When you look for words in a pile of tiles, don't stop with the root: Think about all the possibilities in a single word tile.

One thing Magnetic Poetry® can do is build new words out of spare parts—you can take a bunch of word tiles and put them together to make up new words.

For example, stick **am** and **use** together and you get **amuse**. Add an **r** to **ing** and you get **ring**. You can even make a word out of single letters, such as **ray**.

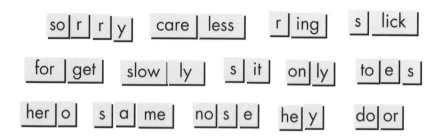

so|r|r|y    care | less    r | ing    s | lick

for | get    slow | ly    s | it    on|ly    to|e|s

her|o    s|a|me    no|s|e    he|y    do|or

Keep a list of "versa-tile" words, like the examples above, as you discover them—they'll come in handy. Here are some "versa-tile" poems:

fire | fly | wait |ing| for
the | dark | ink |y| night
out | of| no|where
off |er |ing| his | light

the | bright | might |y| fly | will
always| be| a |do| red | so
I | put | him | in | a | jar
where | I | keep | him | store |d|

d|e|a|r| s|is
for |give| me| for|
we|a|ring| your | sweat |er|

I | eat | or|e|o|s| in| one| bit |e

# A Grab Bag of Poems

Y ou can write a poem about anything—what you ate for lunch, the smell of your locker, flying along on your skates or your bike, or just staring out the window. You can write a poem about people who don't exist or make-believe places and events. You can be funny or get revenge or tell a secret.

After you've decided what to write about, you can pick the package it comes in. Poems come in all shapes and sizes.

## Jump Starts for Your Brain

Poets use jump starts to limber up their poetry-writing muscles. Each jump start that follows will tell you exactly what to do. Your mission: to follow orders as completely as possible. Who knows? You may write your best poem yet.

# ACTIVITY | self-portrait poem

What makes you distinctively you?
Write a poem in which you describe
yourself—what you look like, how you act.
Go into detail, but try to capture the basic
ingredients of yourself in just a few lines.

me

I am perfect

I ride stallion s

I live like a queen

I don't like to be seen

I ride in a mini van

I am normal

ERIN GANNON (age 12)

# ACTIVITY | impossible poem

Ask yourself a question that can't be answered—
then answer it. (Since the question is impossible,
you can say anything you want.) Or, describe
an impossible object. On the following page are
some impossible questions.

- **Where does your shadow live?**
- **What do dogs dream about?**
- **Do fish have a sense of humor?**
- **How much does a dream weigh?**

a | dream | weigh | s

more | than | wish | es

and | less | than | fear | s

---

ACTIVITY  **warning  &  advice  poem**

$\mathrm{Give}$ advice—like how to stay out of
trouble, or how to twirl without getting dizzy,
or how to eat a melting ice-cream cone.
You can also write warnings. The warnings
can be silly or serious, or both. Here are two
warning poems:

*Permit me to warn you*
*against this automobile rushing to*
     *embrace you*
*with outstretched fender*

> CHARLES REZNIKOFF has
> found an elegant way to
> say "watch out."

*Now listen, you watermelons—*
*if any thieves come—*
*turn into frogs!*

> This Japanese poem by ISSA
> is a haiku. Learn more about
> haiku on pages 19–20.

13

ACTIVITY **l i s t  p o e m**

Write a poem made up of:
- **Three things that drive you crazy**
- **Three things you love most**
- **Three things you really hate**
- **The three ugliest things in the world**
- **The three loveliest things in the world**
- **The three saddest things in the world**

**Here's a poem about hated things:**

ACTIVITY **f o o d  p o e m**

Make up a recipe for love (or for anything—try to list the ingredients as well as the directions).
- **Make up a disgusting menu.**
- **Write about the most expensive food in the world.**
- **Write about a certain kind of food without naming it—see if others can guess what it is.**

**Here's a recipe for happiness:**

> *Mix friends*
> *and summer*
> *into swimming pool*
> *and stir.*
> *Add ice cream,*
> *spreading evenly.*
> *Sprinkle jokes*
> *on top.*

ACTIVITY **lies, secrets & fears**

Write a poem made up of lies. Write a poem made up of secrets. Write a poem made up of fears. Here's an example of a poem that lies:

> *My tongue goes out walking*
> *late every night.*
> *It rolls up like a tire*
> *and talks to itself,*
> *And then before dawn, it*
> *climbs back in my mouth.*
> *You taste funny, I say.*
> *Where have you been?*

ACTIVITY | **phrase poem**

Start with a phrase and see where it takes you:

- I remember . . .
- I dream . . .
- I wish . . .
- I see . . .
- I hear . . .
- I don't understand . . .
- When I'm alone . . .
- In the night . . .

**Here's an example:**

I don't understand why
pepper make s you sneeze
and onion s make you cry
why rain fall s down
and grass grow s up
and what hold s up the sky

ACTIVITY **i n n e r   s p a c e   m o n s t e r**

Build a beast, mold a monster, or fashion a fantasy creature. Describe your creation as wildly as you can. Here's a beginning:

| twisted | rope | hair | cover | ing |

| brown | sausage | eyebrow | s | above |

| snake | eye | marble | s | star | ing | from |

| a | squash | ed | melon | head | a | top |

| a | needle | bone | neck |

## By the Numbers

Certain kinds of poems can be like puzzles or games. They must have a certain number of words or syllables in each line. You write, count, fiddle around, add up your totals, and presto—a poem.

ACTIVITY | **many tankas**

A tanka is a poem with five lines. Each line contains a certain number of syllables, which go like this: 5-7-5-7-7. Here's an example:

5   | I | remember | when |

7   | bear | s | made | me | scared | I | saw | one |

5   | on | TV | he | was |

7   | snarl | ing | and | fierce | chasing | kid | s |

7   | just | like | me | and | he | ate | them |

ACTIVITY | **crazy for lunes**

A lune has three lines and counts words instead of syllables. The first line has three words; the second line has five words; the third line has three words. When you write a lune, you'll see that it looks like the moon (well, sort of—use your imagination). And that's where it gets its name—lune is the French word for moon. Here's an example:

3   | number | two | pencil |

5   | scratch | ing | on | paper | like | a |

3   | sniff | ing | yellow | cat |

## ACTIVITY | lanterns alight

A lantern counts words, too. It's a five-line poem whose word count goes like this: 1-3-5-3-1. Use your imagination, squint at the page when you're done, and you'll see that your poem looks like a lantern.

Here's an example:

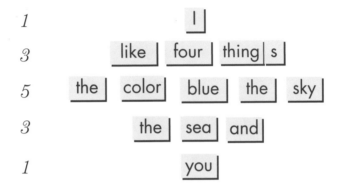

1      I

3      like four thing s

5      the color blue the sky

3      the sea and

1      you

## ACTIVITY | you and haiku

Haiku is a Japanese form of poetry that's usually translated into 17 syllables in three lines. The first line is five syllables; the second line, seven; and the third line, five. Haiku describe small moments or ordinary events. Nature is often the subject.

5   rain | drop | s | on | my | skin

7   freckle | s | that | for | got | to | wear

5   their | brown | color | ed | shell

*Old Pond,*
  *frog jumps in—*
    *plop!*

BASHŌ wrote this poem
more than 300 years
ago. In Japanese, it is
17 syllables long.

---

ACTIVITY | **o n e - t w o - t h r e e   p o e m s**

Write **a poem in which the first line is
made up of one-syllable words, the second
line of two-syllable words, and the third line
of three-syllable words. If you're up for it, try
a four-syllable-word line. Here's an example:**

*1*   I | heard | my

*2*   purple | flannel

*3*   pajama | s | whispering

*4*   inflammable | !

Before you leave this chapter, here are a few more grab bag poems from around the country.

bouquet bomb s away
show er me
bruising blossom s

KITTY O'NEIL

who like s question s
I do not like them
they make me mad
do not ask
any

YASHIRA PABEY (age 12)

a rock is to a garden
as boy s are to life

ARIEL GRUBE

# Details, Details

A poem paints pictures in our heads. It uses words to make those pictures, and that's called imagery. When we write, where do we find these images? From everything we've ever done and seen and heard and smelled and tasted and touched. From our memory. From the things we pay attention to.

## It's All in the Details

Try describing your favorite piece of clothing. Let's say it's a T-shirt. How can you describe that shirt so we'd pick it out of a lineup? What can you say about how it smells and feels, its color and shape and design? Where did you get it? What does it remind you of? Be *specific*—get down to details.

ACTIVITY | **a model-t**

Write your T-shirt poem. Be sure to use the words you've just thought up to describe it. You can shape your poem like a T-shirt, or just write a list of words that capture its essence. Make your T-shirt a mystery object and see if others can guess what it is. There's an example on the next page.

Remember when the car door slammed and everybody said how lucky it was my T-shirt ripped and not my finger? Remember when I spilled a whole glass of grape juice down your used-to-be-white front? We can't be seen in public anymore. But thanks for saving my finger, and I hope you like purple.

## Connecting the Dots

One way to come up with great images is to link two things that normally don't belong together. For instance, you can compare **worry** to **a knotted rope,** or **jealousy** to **a feather stuck in your throat,** or **a dog's bark** to **an old man's cough.** All kinds of things can be compared: feelings, senses, objects, people, events. The best images surprise us by being clear and sharp, weird and funny, so we can *see* what the poet is describing, as if we'd never noticed it before.

# 1.

One way to **compare** two things is by using the words **like** and **as**. Think about how two different things could be alike. Take anger, for instance. Is it hot, like fire? Cold as an ice cube? As bitter as medicine? Can anger be scary, like being lost in fog? There are all kinds of anger—and depending on which kind you're writing about (let your mind wander and see what connections you come up with), you'll find an image to match what you mean.

## ACTIVITY | as like is like

Using the words like **and** as, **see how many connections you can make between two different things. Here are some examples:**

you | dance | like | a | hot | bug |

the | letter | T | is | like | a | weight | lift |er|

he | chew| s | like | a | steam | shovel |

a | whisper | tickle | s | like | butt| er | fly | wing| s |

his | pant| s | are | as | big | as | a | base|ball| stadium |

my | school| look| s | like | an | ice | cube | tray |

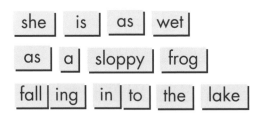

she | is | as | wet |
as | a | sloppy | frog |
fall | ing | in | to | the | lake |

Compare this poem to
BASHŌ's on page 20.

*Mom's mashed potatotes taste like dirty socks,*
*Her instant oatmeal tastes like instant box,*
*And if she made a pound cake,*
*And she dropped it on your foot,*
*You'd think that it was half a ton of rocks.*

JUDITH VIORST, longtime
author and poet, serves up
similies that make us laugh
at ourselves.

## Straight to the Point

**2.** You can be even more **direct** when you compare things *without* using either **like** or **as.** Then you are saying that two completely different things *are* the same. On the next page are some examples.

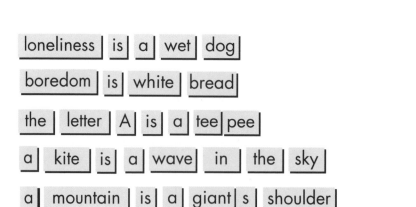

loneliness | is | a | wet | dog

boredom | is | white | bread

the | letter | A | is | a | tee | pee

a | kite | is | a | wave | in | the | sky

a | mountain | is | a | giant | s | shoulder

boats | are | shoe | s | and | sail | s | are | sock | s

---

**ACTIVITY** | **is it? it is**

Pick a group of word tiles. Choose ones that trigger strong feelings or memories. Make sure you've got a variety of words— feelings, objects, people. For example:

dream | window | summer | joy | water | cry

love | monster | dark | silent | morning

Choose a word from the list of words you made. Think about it (it helps to close your eyes). What do you see? What pictures pop into your mind? Write down everything you can think of, whether it makes sense or not. Now pick from the list the images (comparisons) you like best and put them together in a poem.

CITY

*In the morning the city*
*Spreads its wings*
*Making a song*
*In stone that sings.*

*In the evening the city*
*Goes to bed*
*Hanging lights*
*About its head.*

This poem by LANGSTON HUGHES draws a peaceful portrait of New York City.

## Bring It to Life

**3.** Poets often write about lifeless objects or feelings as if they were **alive**. Say you're looking out the window and see tree branches dancing in the wind. Well, they're not really dancing, of course, but the branches do look like arms and they're moving in a graceful way, which reminds you of dancing. So that's the word you would use—if you were writing about trees, that is.

Poems can bring all kinds of things to life—pizza and telephones and T-shirts—by giving them living qualities. For instance, you could write a poem about a backpack that talks back. Guess what—it's sick and tired of lugging around your books. It can't stand those clanking key chains—it much prefers patches. One more thing—its straps are tired!

## as if

Look around your room and find something that has feelings or a story to tell. Your sneakers probably have a lot of personality. So do your socks—not to mention your bed, body parts, stuffed animals and toys, pets, computer, refrigerator, and the family car. Choose an object and bring it to life. See how many human qualities you can give it.

### THE GARDEN HOSE

*In the gray evening*
*I see a long green serpent*
*With its tail in the dahlias.*

*It lies in loops across the grass*
*And drinks softly at the faucet.*

*I can hear it swallow.*

You can easily envision what BEATRICE JANOSCO is describing in this poem even without the title as a clue.

Lots of times when you make a comparison, the first phrase that pops into your mind is one you've heard a million times before. You know—expressions such as,

These phrases are called clichés (klee-SHAYS). Avoid them like the plague (speaking of clichés!). Think up new ways of describing, ways that sound fresh and totally your own.

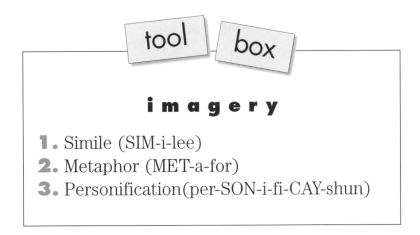

tool box

**i m a g e r y**

**1.** Simile (SIM-i-lee)
**2.** Metaphor (MET-a-for)
**3.** Personification(per-SON-i-fi-CAY-shun)

# Picture This!

P oetry often goes well with a picture. Poetry often *is* a picture! Yes, you can make a poem that looks like something, a poem that moves or reads up, down, and every which way. Here's why: to break out of boring old ways of looking at words on a page; to emphasize the subject or meaning of your poem; to have fun; to drive your readers crazy.

ACTIVITY | **tough stuff**

Concrete **poems are shaped like what they describe. You arrange the words to make a picture of what you're writing about. Here are some examples:**

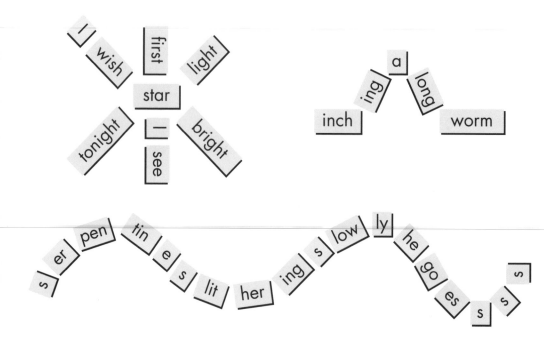

If you're stuck for a shape for your concrete poem, try the outlines provided. You can use word tiles to outline the picture, or fill it in with tiles. You can add to the picture, too.

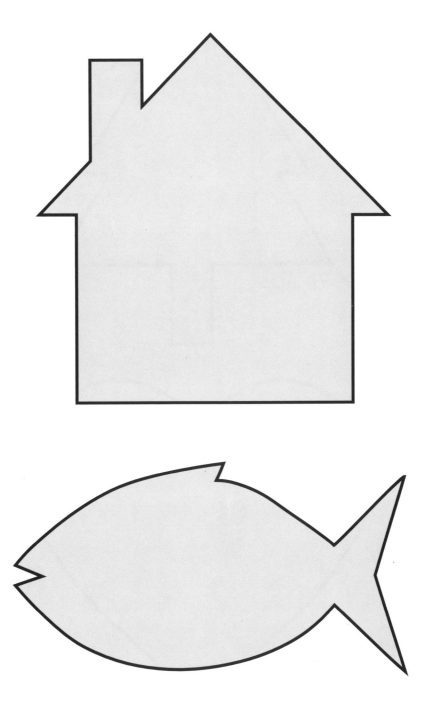

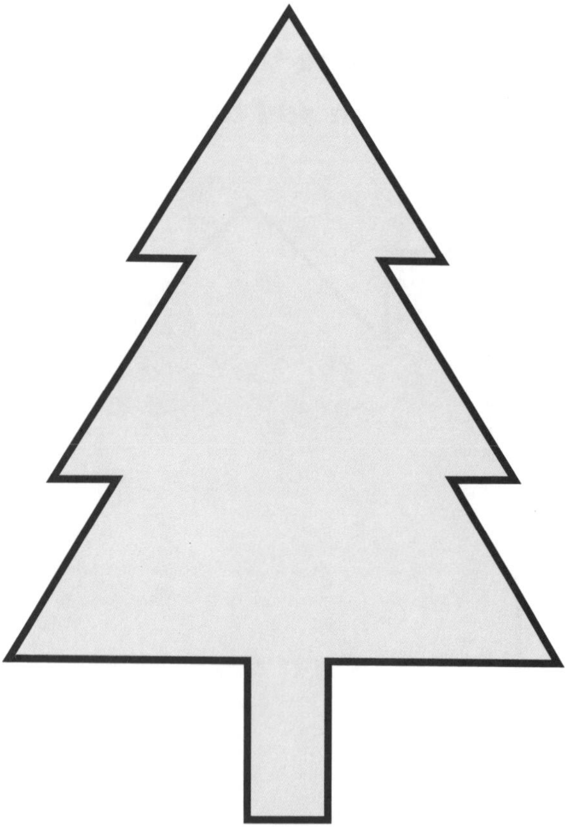

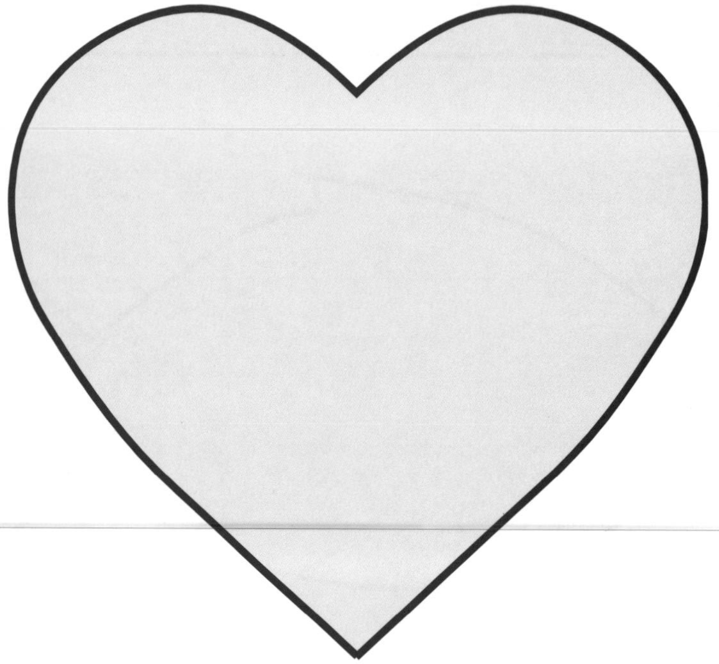

ACTIVITY | **scrambled sgeg**

Maybe you don't want your poem to be so obvious. Maybe you want it to be a puzzle, so the reader has to do some work and guess what's going on. In that case, scramble your letters and words, then scatter them across the page. Try to do it in a way that gives a clue to the poem's meaning. Here's an example:

wind      shield

wipe      rs

s m e a r e d

b'u g e s

bounce | y |

roll | ing | stroll | ing |

not | even | know | ing |

up | or | down | or | all |

around | boil | ed | soft |

egg | s | boil | ed | hard |

sick | pure | never | sure |

expression | lack | ing |

stay | ing | sway | ing |

white |

ERIN GANNON (age 12)

ACTIVITY | **talking magheads**

Use the magnetic shapes in the pouch to make faces that talk. What are they saying? They're reciting poems, of course, but you'll have to put the words in their mouths. See what kind of poem the faces inspire.

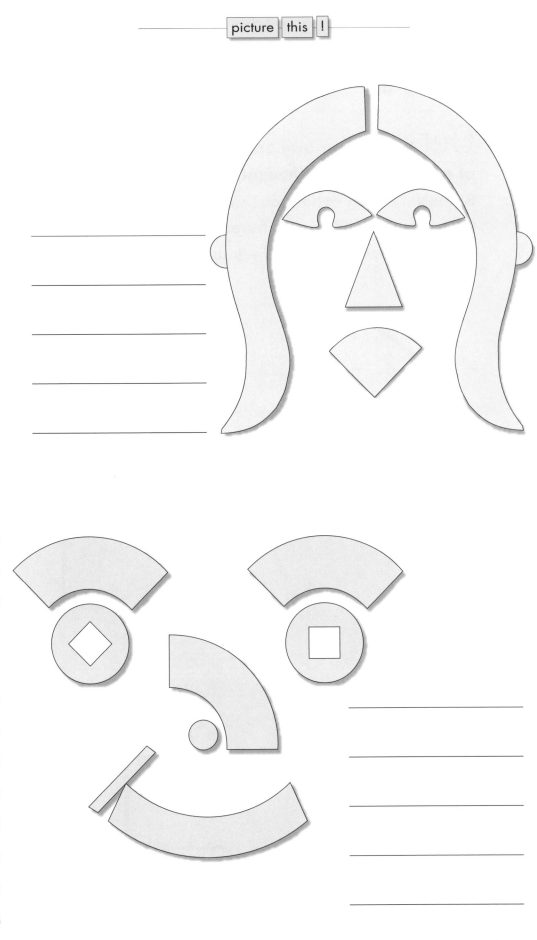

_____

_____

_____

_____

_____

_____

ACTIVITY **out of my mind**

Get inside your own brain. Fill a drawing of a head with your thoughts and feelings. Sometimes the head (you) will be crammed with words, spilling out, bursting from the top. Sometimes your brain-gauge will point

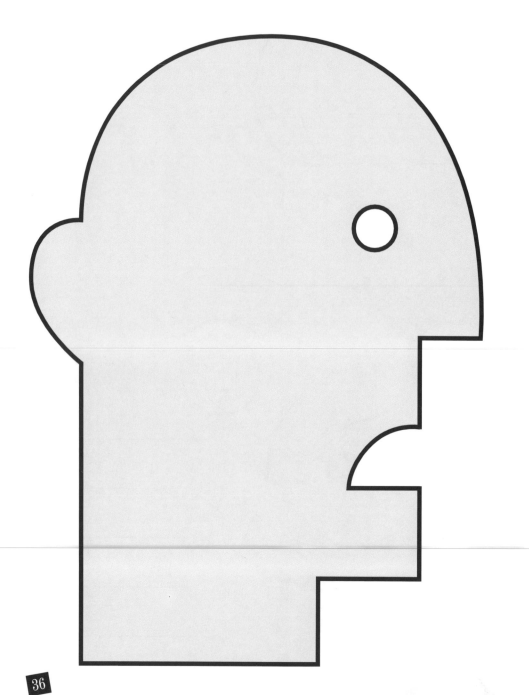

to empty, and there'll be just a few words inside—one word, even. The way you arrange the words can show how you're feeling— bored in a straight line, confused and going in circles, or frustrated, with words stuck at the top of your head, unable to get out. The poem is like an X ray taking a picture of the thoughts and feelings inside your head.

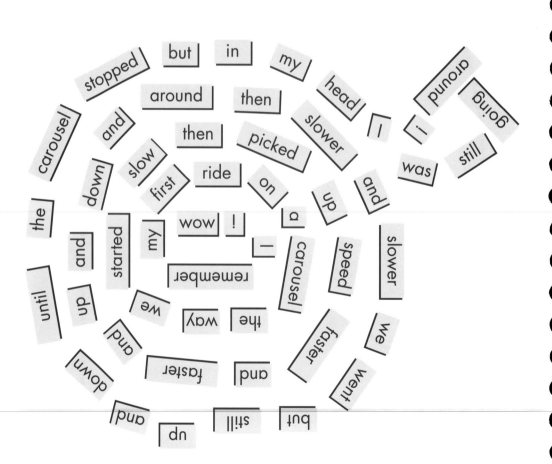

ACTIVITY | **totally loopy**

Write a poem whose words go right to left, or in spirals, or backwards, or upside down, or in all directions like spokes in a wheel, or in a circle so that the poem begins where it ends and never stops.  Make a poem that can be read backwards, forwards, up, or down. Create one that branches out and can be read in more than one way, depending on which path you take through the words.

# Rhythm & Rhyme

**P**oems and songs are a lot alike. Both have rhythm and many have rhyme. Get rid of a song's tune and you've got a poem, tapping out a beat.

## Speak to the Beat

Beat or rhythm: It's the same thing. Some poems have a rhythm pattern so strong, you can pick it up in a minute. But sometimes a poem's rhythm is harder to find; at first it doesn't even seem to be there. The words sound ordinary, like everyday speech. But listen closely and you'll find a musical pattern.

ACTIVITY | **tappity-tap**

As you talk, pay attention to the beat of your words—how do they sound? Tap out their rhythm with your hand, tapping harder on each dark syllable, like this:

I **can't** be**lieve** I **passed** the **test.**

**See** you **la**ter, **al**ligator.

**Give** me a **break.**

**1.** Every word in a poem is chosen not only for its meaning but also for how it sounds—by itself and along with other words. The musical sound of all the words in a poem—that's **rhythm**.

### HALFWAY DOWN

*Halfway down the stairs*
*Is a stair*
*Where I sit.*
*There isn't any*
*Other stair*
*Quite like*
*It.*
*I'm not at the bottom,*
*I'm not at the top;*
*So this is the stair*
*Where*
*I always*
*Stop.*

A. A. MILNE, creator of Winnie-the-Pooh and Christopher Robin, wrote rhythms meant to be read aloud.

Some of the syllables are light, some are heavy. Some sound long, others sound short.

# chants & cheers

We often combine rhyme, rhythm, and repetition to build up steam, shout out good luck, boost our team with cheers, or heckle the other team with jeers. Or we chant for luck, or to remember something important.

*Rah, Rah*
*Sis Boom Bah*
*Push 'em back, Push 'em back*
*WAAAAY back!*

*Rain, rain, go away.*
*Come again some other day.*

## Make up your own chant for anything you like. Then shout it out. Here's an example:

go | glue | !

stick | y |
tack | y |
dry | ing |
slow |
thick |
and |
white |
dry | ing |
tight |

LAURA FOXGROVER (age 10)

## BUFFALO DUSK

*The buffaloes are gone,*
*And those who saw the buffaloes are gone.*
*Those who saw the buffaloes by thousands and how*
*they pawed the prairie sod into dust with their great*
*hoofs, their great heads down pawing on in a*
*great pageant of dusk,*
*Those who saw the buffaloes are gone.*
*And the buffaloes are gone.*

Repetition has its own
beauty, as in this poem
by CARL SANDBURG.

## Rhyme Time

**2.** You know **rhyme**—you hear it all
the time. When words sound alike—**cool
fool school pool rule tool drool**—we say they
rhyme. There are all kinds of rhyme. True rhymes
sound exactly alike, like the words shown above.

**3.** Other rhymes can be **close** but not
exact. These words are close rhymes to the
words shown above: **cruel duel mule ridicule.**
Another kind of close rhyme changes the length of the
word or the ending: **line design remind time.**

Your poems don't have to rhyme in order to be good. In fact, most modern poetry does not rhyme at all. Forcing your poems to rhyme can make them sound as if you chose words just because they rhymed and not because they were right. But still, rhymed poems can be fun to read and fun to write. So if rhyming is up your alley, go ahead and rhyme yourself silly. You can rhyme words at the end of lines, in the middle, or both.

### LIFE DOESN'T FRIGHTEN ME

*Shadows on the wall*
*Noises down the hall*
*Life doesn't frighten me at all*
*Bad dogs barking loud*
*Big ghosts in a cloud*
*Life doesn't frighten me at all*

*I go boo*
*Make them shoo*
*I make fun*
*Way they run*
*I won't cry*
*So they fly*
*I just smile*
*They go wild*
*Life doesn't frighten me at all.*

Take the time to listen to the poet MAYA ANGELOU on tape or in person at a reading.

ACTIVITY | **w o r d   s w a p**

**For the following poem, see what happens when you substitute the bold-faced words with your own words. Or, take any poem you like and swap the rhyming words with your own selection.**

### WET DOG

*Here are instructions*
*for* **washing** *your* **dog.**
**Pick** *a big* **stick,**
*throw it into a* **lake,**
*see him* **swim** *after it*
*(watch out for* **snakes!***)*
**lather** *him* **fast** *when he*
**shakes** *off at your* **feet,**
*Now* **several** *more* **tosses,**
*it's* **rinse cycle,** *repeat*
*the* **thrown stick** *'til*
*he's* **shiny** *and* **clean,**
*then* **dry, hug,** *and* **pet** *him,*
*and* **eat** *some* **ice cream.**

## Break It Up

**4.** Sometimes **the lines** in poems go on and on. Sometimes they're short. How long should each line in your poem be? It depends on which words are important, and on how fast or slow you want the reader to go. Every poem has natural breaks and pauses. When you need to take a breath, that's often a good place to end your line. But breaking the line in unusual and surprising places gives a clue about the meaning of your poem. Here's an example:

### NIGHT CREATURE

*I like*
*the quiet breathing*
*of the night,*

*the tree talk*
*the wind-swish*
*the star light.*

*Day is*
*glare-y*
*loud*
*scary.*
*Day bustles.*

*Night rustles.*
*I like*
*night.*

The short lines of LILIAN MOORE's poem give it the rhythm of breathing.

ACTIVITY **breathtaking verses**

Take a poem. Write it over a few times. **Each time, break up the lines in different places. Read each version out loud. See which one you like best.**

**You can string out the words in one long line, or put a single word on each line, or clump words together. The way you arrange the words and break the lines will shift the meaning. Here's an example:**

*My mother says, don't burp or spit or talk with your mouth full or interrupt or eat with your fingers or drop your fork on the floor.*

*My mother says,*
*don't*
*burp or*
*spit or*
*talk with your*
*mouth full or*
*inter-*
*rupt or*
*eat with your*
*fingers or*
*drop*
*your*
*fork*
*on*
*the*
*floor.*

## WE REAL COOL

### The Pool Players. Seven at the Golden Shovel

*We real cool. We*
*Left school. We*

*Lurk late. We*
*Strike straight. We*

*Sing sin. We*
*Thin gin. We*

*Jazz June. We*
*Die soon.*

Poet GWENDOLYN BROOKS wrote this over forty years ago, but it sounds as up-to-date as when it was new.

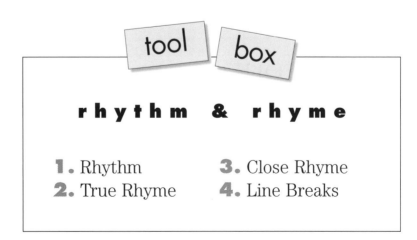

## tool box

### r h y t h m   &   r h y m e

**1.** Rhythm  **3.** Close Rhyme
**2.** True Rhyme  **4.** Line Breaks

# Game Poems

P oetry can be made by a group—that's called fun. Get together with a friend or three and try these poetry-making games.

ACTIVITY **scramble poems**

Get **together with a bunch of friends. Pick fifteen word tiles and spread them out. Have each person in the group write a poem using the same fifteen words. Write each one down as you go along and read them aloud when you've finished. See how different they are.**

ACTIVITY **go 'round poems**

Up to four **people can play. Have each person pick out ten words from the pouch and keep them in a pile. The person who goes first puts down a word from his or her pile. The next person puts a word next to it, and so it goes, each person adding a word to the line/sentence/poem. When all players have used up their words, you've got a poem!**

ACTIVITY **automatic poems**

You can do this by yourself or with a friend. Set a time limit of five minutes. Then, going as fast as you can, take as many words as you can from the pouch and arrange them into a poem. There are no rules. You can put the words down however you like—in short pairs or long phrases. Stack them on top of each other like blocks. String them along as far as you can go. Don't think—just do it! When your time is up, see what you've got.

ACTIVITY **jigsaw poems**

Write a poem using every single word in the pouch. Pile on the plurals, make up new words, stick ing wherever you like. It's like cleaning out the fridge—use everything up!

ACTIVITY | **a c r o s t i c   p o e m s**

Puzzle **lovers will enjoy this form. Here's how it works: Pick a word that triggers ideas in your head. It could be a person's name, or just an ordinary word, like** cool **or** cry **or** ocean. **Spell the word down the left side of a page, starting a new line with each letter of the word.**

Write **a poem that describes the word. Here are some examples:**

> **F**lowery notes,
> **L**ight trills and then, a
> **U**nison burst of applause from
> **T**he audience.
> **E**ncore!

> **P**erfectly delicious, an
> **I**talian delight.
> **Z**ealous chefs toss the dough to give our pizza
> **Z**est. So eat it
> **A**ll!
>
> LAURA FOXGROVER (age 10)

# Extra! Extra!

There's more about poetry than we could ever fit into one book, but we'll try anyway.

## Off the Wall

Every April, magnetic walls are put up all across the country in celebration of National Poetry Month. Here is just a small sampling of the poems we received from walls around the country.

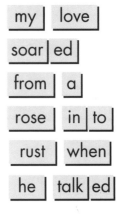

my love
soar ed
from a
rose in to
rust when
he talk ed

BROOKLYN, NY

see a TV on the out side
in side is magic fun dream s
and friend s

SEATTLE, WA

I have garden s in side of me

BLUE BELL, PA

turtle wing and translucent balloon fly slow ly together
smoke upon silent stream
at morning thunder whisper s

NEW YORK, NY

talk child
scream music
play peace
leave dark
live summer
start funny

SEATTLE, WA

remember the
voice in the breeze
and
the wild
vermilion fire
in my eye

MINNEAPOLIS, MN

the sea wind s trudge and blow

SEATTLE, WA

we lie smooth a picture
of honey moon s and beauty and easy
moment s like a light mist after a storm

EVANSTON, IL

where is the chocolate ?
whisper ed the big glow ing sun

BROOKLYN, NY

## Poetalk

Your poetry will speak for itself if you photocopy and cut out these speech balloons. Your word tiles will hold them to a refrigerator door or any magnet-friendly surface.

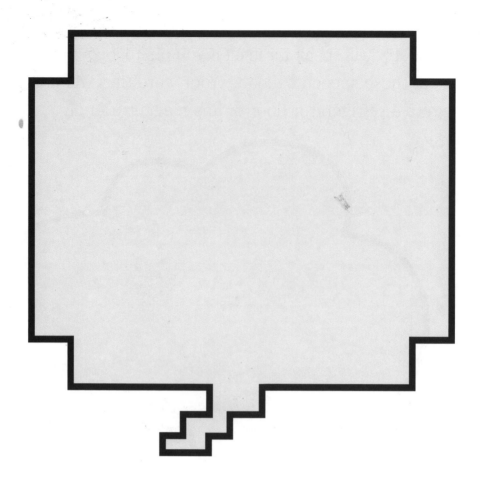

## more words, more poetry

Are you having fun? We hope so. And we know one thing for certain—you'll need more word tiles to say everything that's in your head and heart. If you can't find the Magnetic Poetry® kits you need in your local stores, if you have ideas for new words or kits, or if you want to share your poems for future Magnetic Poetry® publications, call or write us. Here's the address and phone number. We've got a Web site and E-mail, too.

Magnetic Poetry
404 N. Washington Avenue #101
Minneapolis, MN 55401

1-800-370-7697
www.magneticpoetry.com